At Your Service

CHALLENGING AND EQUIPPING YOU TO RE-THINK YOUR WORSHIP STRATEGY

John Leach with Mark Earey

Contents

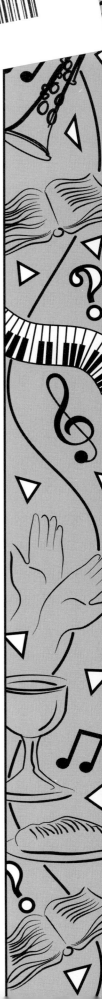

Copyright © 1997 CPAS

First edition 1997
All rights reserved. The material in this book is copyright and may not be photocopied without permission from CPAS. However, permission is given for the owner of this book to copy pages for use in study or discussion groups in which he or she is participating.

Published by CPAS
Athena Drive
Tachbrook Park
WARWICK
CV34 6NG

Editorial and design by AD Publishing Services
Illustrations by Taffy Davies
Printed by Unigraph Printing Services

The initiative for this workbook came from a working group for the Anglican Evangelical Assembly in 1995, co-ordinated by Clare Wells. Church of England Evangelical Council is the umbrella organization for the Anglican Evangelical Assembly.

ISBN 1 8976 6078 2
British Library Cataloguing-in-Publication Data
A catalogue record for this book is available from the British Library

Church Pastoral Aid Society
Registered Charity No 1007820
A company limited by guarantee

Introduction

I like to think of myself as a bit of a musician. I *feel* like a musician. Music affects how I spend my time and money, how I think, how my emotions respond, and so on. But it's when I get together with others to play that I'm *really* a musician. Those are special times when we focus together on music, and actually produce something as a result.

I also like to think of myself as a worshipper. That too affects my whole outlook on life. I seek constantly to live out St Paul's instruction to offer myself as a living sacrifice, holy and pleasing to God, which is my spiritual act of worship. But something special happens when I meet with other worshippers specifically to focus on giving worship to God. Yes, the whole of life is worship, but it finds its central focus in the corporate worship of the church week by week.

This workbook is about those meetings for corporate worship. Today, most of the denominations in Britain are declining in numbers. Whatever we have been doing in worship, at least on a human level, just hasn't been working. Not only have we failed to draw others into the worshipping community, we haven't even been able to hold on to those who are already in. Of course what really matters is what God thinks, not what we think, but can he really be pleased with a church whose central purpose seems to have become so alienating?

We are also in a time of change. As an Anglican I use a prayer book which to some extent is already out of date after only seventeen years, but which replaced one which had lasted for over 300 years. It seems that a growing realization of the need for change has coincided with a much faster rate of change.

It is therefore a good time to produce a workbook which encourages us to take a long hard look at the worship of our churches. Its aim is neither to condemn what we do, nor to push us into inappropriate forms of worship, but rather to help us face some uncomfortable truths and to take steps to do things better.

Mark and I are both Anglican vicars, although I was brought up as a Baptist, and have worked in an Anglican-Baptist Local Ecumenical Project (LEP). Mark, who contributed Chapter 3, has also served in an Anglican-Methodist LEP. Therefore, while our language may at times show our Anglican bias, we have tried as much as possible to make this workbook accessible to Christians of all denominations and of all worship styles. We are both interested in worship, and have written about it on occasions, but we are first and foremost working ministers of churches which face the

same sort of problems as everyone else. To save long lists of alternatives, we have referred to the main decision-making group in the church as the 'church council'.

The workbook consists of five chapters; each has an introductory section which seeks to get you thinking around the subject, followed by some suggested discussion topics and group exercises. Just who will use it is a matter for you to decide. Perhaps the minister and one or two other people should read through it and then work more carefully through it, over an extended period, with a larger group. It could be used as a study project for the whole church council or a sub-group of it. You could create a special 'worship group' to consider it and report back. Or the whole congregation might work at it, for example in a series of Lent home groups. But however it is handled, it will take time; it would be wise to allow at least a couple of sessions for each of the five chapters, and more if issues arise which need more lengthy consideration.

However, you should be clear what this workbook will not do for you.

- **It will not tell you everything is all right:** rather it will encourage you, without condemning you, to be realistic in facing those areas where change is necessary and maybe even long overdue.

- **It will not solve all your problems:** it will probably give you more problems, at least in the short term! But they will be creative problems of growth.

- **It will not tell you how you ought to be worshipping:** it will encourage you to think that out for yourself, so that your pattern and methods are right for your church.

- **It will not push a particular line:** it will seek to speak to, and ask questions of, all sorts of traditions.

- **It will not demand to be used in a particular way, or presuppose any 'right' answers:** it is simply a tool which you can use as is appropriate for you.

- **It will not completely revolutionize the worship of your church overnight:** however, it may help to do so longer term!

- **Above all, it will not give you a blueprint for your church's worship,** but it will encourage you to think about creating a strategy for renewing your worship.

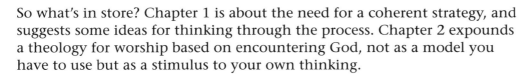

So what's in store? Chapter 1 is about the need for a coherent strategy, and suggests some ideas for thinking through the process. Chapter 2 expounds a theology for worship based on encountering God, not as a model you have to use but as a stimulus to your own thinking.

Chapter 3 explains how to use (and how not to use) a worship audit. If the suggestion convinces you, it will be worth researching it further and even carrying out the audit before continuing with this workbook. Or you may like to finish reading the book and then revisit the two final chapters after your audit, with all the new insights that it will bring.

Finally, there are two chapters on handling change. Chapter 4 is about creating a church climate in which change can be embraced more readily, and Chapter 5 is about the actual implementation of your strategy.

Obviously, those who are to take part in the discussion and activities will need to have read the introductory material first, and any changes which result will need to be handled within the legal or constitutional framework of your particular denomination, but apart from that there are no rules. We hope you enjoy the workbook, and that you can let God use it to enhance your week-by-week worship, so that the worship of all God's people may be offered in ways that are pleasing to him and glorifying to his name.

John Leach
Mark Earey

CHAPTER 1

Develop your strategy

What's the problem?

Discontent is in the air. The church council knows that things are not going well. Numbers are down, the offerings are getting smaller, and there is a tired, listless atmosphere hanging over the place. In a massive attempt at honesty, the council is discussing what to do in order to reverse the trend of decay and death. What is needed is *An Idea*.

Suddenly Mabel in the corner springs to her feet. She has just read a book about modern worship, which claimed great things for churches which get it right. 'What we need here,' she exclaims, 'is a Sympathizer!' The church council, relieved beyond telling that *someone* has had a positive idea, quickly

THE MIGHTY SYMPATHIZER

passes a motion that we buy a sympathizer, with only two abstentions, one from Joe who is the only one to admit that he doesn't know what a sympathizer is, and one from the church organist who thinks that our current heating system is perfectly adequate. Thus the church becomes the proud owner of a Roland E16 electronic synthesizer. Unfortunately no one knows how to play it, and sadly the promised revival still tarries while the synth gathers dust in a cupboard, and the council goes off in search of *Another Idea*.

What was lacking, of course, was any sense of *strategy*. Sadly, many churches do limp along from one good idea to the next, never stopping to ask some more fundamental questions along the way. This chapter introduces two tools, or ways of thinking, which may help us to be a little more careful about how we look at the future.

Strategic thinking is a skill which a church and its leadership can learn, but primarily it is an attitude of mind into which we can grow. The tools will help us to begin (or continue) thinking about things in a long-term way rather than simply searching for

the next idea. One church leader has referred to strategic thinking as 'writing your history in advance' and, leaving aside any of God's little surprises along the way, that's not a bad way of looking at it.

However, this is not merely another book on business management techniques. Church leadership (and worship management) clearly does involve thinking; that's why God gave us those grey squidgy things inside our heads. But it isn't about thinking up our own good ideas. God, the master strategist, has his plan and his agenda for our churches: he has his special journey for each one of them to take. So our part in strategizing is simply to discern what is his way for us, his answer to every problem and blockage we encounter, and his mind on every decision we face. Over some things he will be neutral, and like a good loving father he'll ask us, 'What do *you* want to do?' But over others he'll be there to guide and direct us. So right from the start we need to emphasize the place of prayer, reflection and Spirit-led discussion in the strategizing process. This is more than business studies, it's about studying God's business.

CHAPTER 1

Think strategically

First, consider this diagram, gleaned from Bill Beckham, an American church strategist:

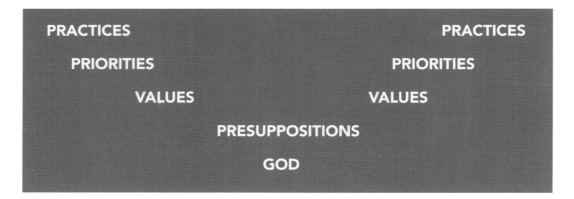

PRACTICES		PRACTICES
PRIORITIES		PRIORITIES
VALUES		VALUES
	PRESUPPOSITIONS	
	GOD	

We start the process at the top with our *Practices*, the things which as a church we actually *do*. We do these things because we don't do other things; in other words our *Practices* depend on our *Priorities*. Most of church life functions on these two levels, and most change in church life is about fiddling with them. Things aren't going well: let's *do* something. Instead of repainting the hall, we'll splash out on a synth. A change in priority has led to a change in practice.

But priorities are not the bottom line. Beneath them lie our *Values*, in other words the things we think and feel are important. No one talked about this level at the church council meeting, but it was clearly of value to them to get out of decline and into growth. Many values are to a high degree neutral. Some churches highly value liturgy, ceremonial and traditional church music; others feel that honouring God through contemporary audio-visual media is their prime task. These are not right or wrong, any more than I am right to have purple as my favourite colour and my wife is wrong to prefer blue; they simply are, as the name suggests, value judgments.

Clearly, though, it's not quite as simple as that. If your church council decided that what would really pull in the crowds would be a revival of the practice from biblical times of temple prostitution, others might question whether or not God would be happy with the idea, and might argue from other parts of the Bible that he'd find it detestable. Some values obviously *might* be 'wrong' and unacceptable, if they conflict with biblical revelation about the

sort of things God approves or forbids. Therefore we need to dig even deeper, to our *Presuppositions*, the things we take for granted due to the information given to us about who God himself is. Thus each of the churches mentioned above have their different values because the Bible or church tradition tells them something about the nature of God; he is to be honoured with the very best choral liturgy, or with worship which is culturally familiar to non-churchgoers. It is because God is so complex and many-faceted that we have so much choice.

So how might change proceed? We need to move up the right hand side of the diagram. The first step must be the articulation of our values. Before leaping to a conclusion, the council could have spent some time asking questions about what was important to them as a church. This in turn could lead to or spring from a discussion of presuppositions: the desire to emerge from the doldrums may have been because they believed in a God of growth and life. A Bible study on the nature of God would

confirm their presupposition that God did indeed expect his church to be alive rather than dying.

Building the strategy can start once the foundations have been dug down to the bedrock. What is God like? How do we know; where does it say that in the Bible? What do we particularly value in his character? Therefore, in the light of all that, what are we going to put our main efforts into, and at the expense of what else? And as the ideas begin to flow, each can be evaluated according to whether or not it fits with the values. If radical change is necessary, you can begin working on changing the values of the church; only when that has happened will practical changes take place smoothly.

Thus there are both practical and theological jobs to do, and they will require careful critical observation and thought as well as prayerful listening to God. These can be the work not just of the minister or leader but of the whole church, or a group delegated to do the work on their behalf.

CHAPTER 1

Plan your journey

My second tool is really just a clarification of terms, which I have found necessary since one hears words used in so many different ways. Having explained my convention, I'll stick to it throughout the rest of this workbook. Imagine a family engaged in planning a summer camping holiday

in France. Before we ever get into the car we need to do some serious thinking.

First of all we have the **Vision**, the collective picture of what the whole holiday is about: three weeks of doing nothing in the sun, with lots of garlic. But then there must be a journey, and to cope with that we need an **Aim**: we want to get to Port Camargue. We know that if we arrive in Carnac there is something wrong. Therefore we need a **Strategy**: which way are we going? There might be several options: the Autoroute du Soleil down the Rhone Valley is direct but expensive, so we could go via Tours and the Dordogne, because we like that area. In one sense it doesn't matter, as long as we achieve our aim of getting to Port Camargue, so we base our

decision on all sorts of factors. But we need one more thing: a set of **Goals** along the way. So we book a campsite at Tours for the first night, and another near Sarlat for the second. Not only does this keep us more or less on the right road, it also lets us know how we're progressing. If we're still on the Paris ring road four days into the holiday we could fairly conclude that we've lost our way.

This comparison is helpful in planning for developing our worship. We probably already have a vague **Vision:** we want to be liturgical and catholic like All Saints' Margaret Street, or spontaneous and charismatic like Anaheim Vineyard, or whatever. So what's the **Aim**: how will we know when we've arrived at our final destination (bearing in mind that long before we get there our view will have clarified and our horizons broadened still further)? What is our **Strategy**: what are we actually going to do which will enable us to reach that aim? And finally, how can we break down that strategy into smaller steps so that we can check our progress? What **Goals** do we hope to have reached, and by when?

> 'Vision is the art of seeing things impossible.'
> *Jonathan Swift*

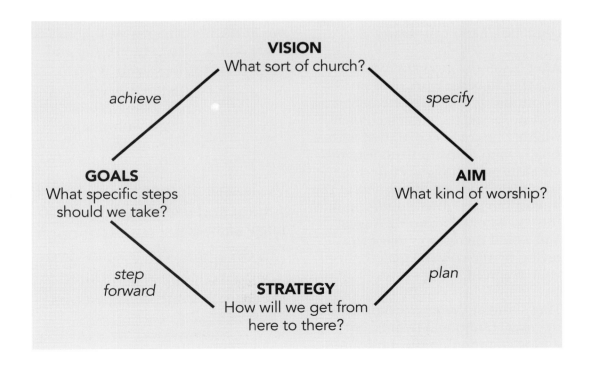

VISION
What sort of church?

achieve   *specify*

GOALS
What specific steps
should we take?

AIM
What kind of worship?

*step
forward*   *plan*

STRATEGY
How will we get from
here to there?

CHAPTER 1

How it worked for one church

One church had a vision for moving from totally organ-based worship to a group of musicians and much 'freer' worship. So they stated an aim: in two years from now we want a good-quality worship team leading worship at our main Sunday service alongside more traditional organ-based hymns.

So what was the strategy? Early in the New Year the minister invited four people who he knew had some musical gifts and an interest in more contemporary worship to a meeting at his home, where he suggested they form a worship team with him. He talked through the sort of thing he wanted to see, played them some examples on CDs, and asked them to consider prayerfully whether they could be a part of the team.

After Easter the group of five met together to begin work on a small repertoire, and at the same time the minister asked the church council whether he could experiment with a small group of instrumentalists and vocalists providing music during the administration of communion in the August services. After promising that this would only be during August, and would then stop subject to a review by the church council, the church agreed.

That summer the services contained the usual traditional hymns, but during communion the musicians, located at the back of the church, led some gentle worship songs, the words of which were printed on the weekly notice sheet. The reaction was largely positive, but, true to his word, the minister returned in September to the previous diet of hymns. By the October church council meeting they were begging him to start the group again. So the process continued, with a carefully thought-out strategy and some specifically timed goals along the way. Two years later the whole ethos of the church's worship had changed. A few people had left, but most were perfectly happy with the mix of musical styles.

So there are some tools and terms to help your thinking along. They will apply to many areas of church life, but in the next chapter we'll home in more on the subject of worship and try to define what exactly it is.

'A vision statement looks to the future, and will stretch us to do what we are not strong enough to do alone. We trust in God for guidance, help, endurance and his Spirit to empower us.'

Peter Brierley, Vision Building, Christian Research, 1994, p 32

Aim

To clarify our vision, and to discover our values, for worship in our church.

1. Bible base

Read the story of Abraham, especially:

- Genesis 12:1-9
- Genesis 15:1-21
- Genesis 16:1-6,15,16
- Genesis 17:1-8,23-27
- Genesis 21:1-7
- Genesis 22:1-19
- Hebrews 11:8-12.

a What was the vision?
b Who gave it?
c How did Abraham react to it?
d How did Abraham (seek to) implement it?
e How was it tested and how did Abraham deal with the test?
f What lessons can you draw for understanding and implementing the vision you have?

2. Identify your values

a List the main values you have as a church – the things of first importance. Then think of five values which you do not have, not because they are bad but because they don't seem right for you, even though other churches might have them with perfect validity. To what extent are the values you've identified those of the whole church, or just of a group within it? What values might other groups within the church hold? Does this lead to conflict? If so, how does the church handle it?

b Visit a church which is very different from yours. What are some of their values? Note down how the things they do flow from their values.

c Think of ways in which the values you've identified could be communicated to church members and visitors, to say something about the 'personality' of your church.

3. Define your vision

Take some time to dream dreams. Write, in 250 words or so, a description of your ideal worship service with every resource you'd wish for. Then tell each other *why* your service would be like this. Also, draft in about fifty words a vision statement to include your aims, your reasons for them, and when you hope to achieve them. Use it as a basis for identifying goals along the way, and share it with your church council or leadership team.

CHAPTER 2

What is worship?

Key elements

The answer to the question: 'What is worship?' depends, of course, on who you ask. Much has been written about it, and many helpful ways of understanding it have been formulated, so I almost hesitate to add another. This chapter (alliterated because it has been written by a preacher) suggests five elements.

Worship is:

- an *Encounter* with God
- beginning with *Exultation*
- which may lead on to *Edification*
- then to *Encouragement*
- and/or *Empowering*.

The idea of this chapter is not to sell you a particular theological line, but to encourage you to think theologically about worship; in that sense it provides a model rather than a blueprint. The real question is: could your church write its own equivalent of this chapter?

Encountering God

Our theology begins with who God is. If you're on a walk and you see a bull in the field, you run. If you hear a funny joke, you laugh. If you see a policeman with his hand up, you stop. It's in the very nature of those things that you respond in a particular way. So it is with God. When you encounter the King of kings, the Ruler of the universe, the loving Father, you worship. As the Anglican liturgy puts it, 'It is *right* to give him thanks and praise'. In fact, according to St Paul, most of the problems of the human race stem from the fact that we have failed to respond appropriately; we have neither glorified him as God, nor

given thanks to him (Romans 1:21).

If you were living in or around Palestine in the Old Testament period, you would have had a great deal of choice about your worship. Quite apart from the varieties of '-ites' listed at odd points in the Bible (Jebusites, Amalekites and the like, who each had their own gods and rituals), you could have gone for Babylonian, Assyrian, Philistine, or any one of many different faiths. But only one of them has survived and evolved to the present day – Hebrew worship led to Judaism and on to Christianity. You won't find any Perizzite temples left – except in

archaeological digs – but in some parts of the world Christianity is expanding all the time.

So what was so special about Hebrew worship which led to its continuation while everything else gradually died out? Theologian Samuel Terrien, in *The Elusive Presence* (San Francisco: Harper and Row, 1978), suggests that it was the only worship which recognized and expected the presence of God among the worshippers. All sorts of people worshipped (and still do worship) a god 'out there' somewhere. The God of Israel, however, was present in the here and now with his worshippers. Of course in Old Testament times they needed help for that presence to become accessible for them; they needed holy places, shrines or temples; holy people, the priests and Levites; and holy times for worship and sacrifice.

But when Jesus came to be the Messiah to the Jewish people and to the whole world, the basis of worship was changed. Through his death on the cross he opened 'a new and living way' to God (Hebrews 10:20). The requirements of the old covenant were 'an annual reminder of sins, because it is impossible for the blood of bulls and goats to take away sins' (Hebrews 10:3,4). But Jesus inaugurated a new covenant offering 'for all time one sacrifice for sins' so that, because forgiveness is freely available, 'there is no longer any [need for] sacrifice for sin' (Hebrews 10:12,18). As a result, through the

Holy Spirit, poured out upon the church, Jesus' followers were made into a kingdom of priests and a spiritual temple. God was present in his worshipping community and in their whole lives.

That was not the end of formal worship, however. Jesus and the apostles met in the temple and synagogues, and later the 'church' met in people's homes for 'teaching and... fellowship, ... the breaking of bread and... prayer' (Acts 2:42). As the church grew, so there grew a need for discipline in worship (1 Corinthians 14:26-33) and authority in ministry (1 Timothy 3:1-13). Later, of course, some of the old divisions crept back in, as church buildings became regarded as holy shrines and church leaders became the only mediators of God's word and grace. Life became divided into worship and everything else.

True worship, of course, reminds us that God is not 'out there': he is close to each one of us. Worship can and should be a meeting with him; while it is our duty to worship, it can and should be our joy, too.

So how does this encounter happen? At times God encounters us, and sometimes to our surprise we find ourselves responding to him in worship. But it is more likely that we will encounter him by coming consciously into his presence and giving him some 'quality time'. That's what church services are about. Whether or not we *feel* that

we have encountered God, the fact that we have attended a service means that we have gone to meet with the King of kings. Also, we have done so corporately, in a way which is qualitatively different from any individual meeting with him at home during the week. Worship is a response to the unchanging character of God irrespective of our changeable feelings.

Other aspects of worship

We give God our time and attention in worship services to *exult* in his presence, and to *exalt* his name. In other words, to enjoy him and to tell him (and others) so. Psalm 96 is one example of a worship song which has this dual focus, a concern to join in with the worship which all creation is rightly and joyfully giving to God, and a call to others to be a part of the celebration. Such worship opens us up to receive from God a fresh infusion of 'every spiritual blessing in Christ' (Ephesians 1:3). Above all, one of the things which 'pleases the Lord' is making 'music in your heart' and 'always giving thanks to God' (Ephesians 5:10,19,20).

Through corporate worship, God desires to *edify* his people, building them up or leading them forward in their discipleship. He may speak to us through the reading and exposition of his word, through the liturgy, sacrament or music, or through a prophetic word or picture. We may have one of those 'Aha!' moments when a lightbulb is suddenly switched on for us, and we see or understand something for the

first time. All this is God's gift of grace to us, and there is nothing we can do to work it up or deserve it. Perhaps it was this kind of experience during the Antioch Church staff meeting which launched Paul's missionary career in Acts 13:1-3.

Even if nothing that earth-shattering happens for us, we may still be encouraged by having been with God's worshipping people. Psalm 92 tells us that it is good to praise the Lord, and even if it has not been life-changing, we can still feel something of the peace, presence and power of God in our anxious or questioning hearts.

And then, of course, we may be *empowered* to live for God after the worship event is over, so that our whole life becomes a sacrifice (the spiritual act of worship demanded by Paul in Romans 12:1). When I'm preaching I always try to encourage people to respond, and to give them space to do so. Often that response is to invite God to enable us to apply what we've heard. Some preaching puts pressure on us to 'perform' in

one way or another; I try instead to encourage people to invite God to equip them 'with everything good for doing his will' and working in them 'what is pleasing to him' (Hebrews 13:21). Of course we need to co-operate, but sometimes 'Christian living' is portrayed as nothing more than human hard work which God is asked to bless. That can be less enjoyable and fruitful than opening ourselves to his empowering as we meet him in worship.

The elements of worship services

What we do in worship is therefore a means to help us meet, or encounter, God.

> The typical 'ingredients' of church worship might include:
>
> ♦ singing hymns and/or songs
> ♦ listening as the Bible is read and expounded
> ♦ offering prayers and praises
> ♦ receiving bread and wine
> ♦ giving financial gifts for God's work
> ♦ hearing the notices which involve us all in the day-to-day life of the body of Christ where we live
> ♦ meditating silently
> ♦ listening to awe-inspiring music
> ♦ sharing stories of God's activity in people's lives
> ♦ symbolic actions, processions, dance, drama
> ♦ liturgical and spontaneous elements.

We all have different likes, dislikes and preferences, and traditionally they have been battlegrounds within churches, but if we can see them as means to a greater end, we can begin to evaluate whether or not they do the job. Thus we might ask, for example, whether listening to the choir chanting Psalm 119 does help us to be encouraged in the Lord, or whether forty-five minutes of charismatic choruses do significantly increase our biblical knowledge or spiritual empowerment. If they do, all well and good, but if they achieve very little for worshippers except perhaps to reinforce the 'feel-good' factor, we might need to consider the possibility that they are approaching the status of idols to which we attach greater importance than we do to meeting God. The means can become more precious than the end.

One more dimension needs consideration. It seems clear from the biblical evidence that what would please God more than anything else would be if everyone on the face of the earth could join in worshipping him, rather than just the relatively small proportion who do at the moment. The Psalms are full of 'calls

We might ask whether forty-five minutes of charismatic choruses do significantly increase our biblical knowledge or spiritual empowerment.

to worship', and the picture of heaven glimpsed in the book of Revelation contains the wholehearted participation of all its citizens in the worship of the Lamb. This raises the question of 'user-friendliness'. It is possible that some of our worship, which genuinely edifies, encourages and empowers *us* is incomprehensible to those who, for a variety of reasons, don't know the things we know or share our background. Jesus had some hard words to say to those who enjoyed their own religious practice while excluding others (for example in Matthew 23:13).

There are two contemporary schools of thought about what creates this user-friendliness. Church A believes that the services need to be stripped of anything which feels 'churchy'. People must be allowed to sit back, relax, and watch a performance

'Worship is the submission of all our nature to God. It is the quickening of conscience by His holiness; the nourishment of mind with His truth; the purifying of imagination by His beauty; the opening of the heart to His love; the surrender of will to His purpose – and all of this gathered up in adoration, the most selfless emotion of which our nature is capable and therefore the chief remedy for that self-centredness which is our original sin and the source of all actual sin.'

William Temple, Readings in St John's Gospel, MacMillan, 1945, p 68

CHAPTER 2

which makes no demands on them, and listen to God's word made strikingly relevant to the real problems which face them in their everyday life. Church B, on the other hand, thinks that it is important for people to experience the power of God moving among them so that his presence meets people in manifestations which may at first seem alien and perhaps a little frightening, but will leave them in no doubt that he is real, powerful and active.

Since both churches have grown significantly, it is an open question as to which approach is the 'right' one. Indeed, some churches have grown by combining both elements, and others have found less dramatic modifications can also be vehicles of God's revelation to church newcomers. You will need to decide which view you subscribe to, since it will affect your strategy dramatically. But whatever your view, it is vital that your worship is attractive to those who at present are outside the worshipping community, if you are to avoid some of Jesus' criticisms of inward-looking groups who only cater for themselves.

So how are we doing with our worship? The next chapter will suggest how we might go about answering that question.

A biblical understanding of worship
Romans 12

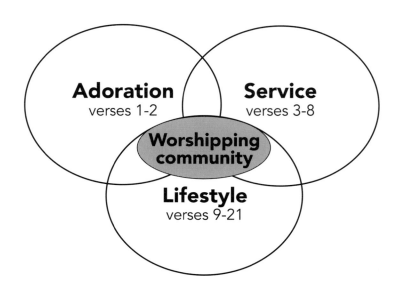

Worship is a two-way experience

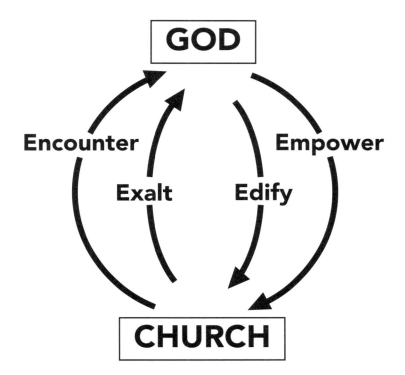

GOD

Encounter   Empower

Exalt   Edify

CHURCH

GROUP FOCUS

Aim

To measure up our understanding of worship against the Bible, and to analyze what helps people to worship God.

1. Bible base

Read Psalms 95, 96, 103. What elements of worship are described? What aspects of God's character are singled out for worship? How might we include these in our worship services?

2. Explain yourself!

One Sunday you are visited at your church by a space alien who has dropped in for your morning service. He is friendly but curious to know what you are all doing. Role-play your explanation of the service, and remember you have a golden opportunity to share your faith with him and to try to lead him to Christian commitment.

3. Listen to each other

Talk together about your most memorable worship experiences. As each of you describes their favourite, you may be hearing something very precious and special, which deserves reverence and respect. You may want to move into some shared silence or open prayer together. Then try to analyze things a little more. In particular, try to spot any common factors which emerge from different people's stories. To what degree was a sense of the 'presence' of God, or an 'encounter' with him significant for people and how was it mediated?

4. Why do you go to church?

All worship is a mixture of what the Anglican liturgy calls 'duty' and 'joy'. What are the kinds of things which make it feel more joyful than dutiful? How do you usually feel as the prospect of going to your own church looms each week?

Worship audit

Evaluating our worship

Everyone has an opinion about the worship they experience at church on Sunday. This is not a problem. The problem is that so few of us feel that what we think about the worship will make any difference to how it will be *next* week.

In many churches the minister makes all the decisions about worship. This is changing slowly. In the Church of England the incumbent is legally required to consult the church council about the pattern of worship services offered. The involvement of lay people in leading services has increased. The organist or other musicians may choose the music. Some churches have a worship committee which shares the task of planning with the church leaders.

However, despite all this, in most churches it's a relatively small number of people who know that their opinion about the worship will make a difference. The majority still have to endure it *without* having their opinion considered. In the long term this can breed a lot of discontent in the congregation and may also mean that the worship itself goes off in an eccentric (and perhaps unbiblical or unhelpful) direction, following the personal preferences of the leaders or committee.

Another problem is that some people express opinions and perhaps even make changes without doing any 'theology' – without thinking about God. It is an alarming fact that most decisions about changes in our worship are taken by a small number of people, on the basis of human preferences and opinions and without hard thought being given to what God himself requires.

Reasons for an audit

We therefore need to evaluate our worship in a way that keeps sight of what God wants, but which also involves the majority of the congregation so that they can 'own' any changes in worship that are made. The risk is that when you *do* give people a chance to express their opinion, you will be buried by an avalanche of frustration built up over many years. No wonder clergy get scared at the idea of evaluating their church's worship. It feels a lot safer to keep the lid firmly *on* this can of worms.

CHAPTER 3

The risk is that when you do give people a chance to express their opinion, you will be buried by an avalanche of frustration built up over many years.

Therefore, if you set out to evaluate your worship, ensure that it is done properly and thoroughly. Worship evaluation done badly or half-heartedly can make matters worse, because it simply confirms and deepens people's prejudices. It also tends to make everyone think that it will make *them* happier with the services, and the result can be very disillusioning.

But if worship really is the prime calling of both the church and the whole of creation, then we should sometimes review the way we do it in church. One way is to conduct a 'Worship Audit'. Like a financial audit, a worship audit allows us to assess honestly where we are, what our assets and liabilities are, and then

allows us to think about where we should be and how things can be improved. A good worship audit forces us to consider *God's* priorities as well as our own. It will clarify our vision, help us to articulate our strategy, and suggest goals to target along the way.

You can hold an 'audit' (or 'review') of your worship in many different ways. What is important is to plan it, and if possible to involve someone (or a group) from outside your own congregation – an outside consultant who can bring a fresh but sympathetic eye and ear to all that happens. Many churches, and some Church of England dioceses, have already begun a programme of worship audit, and one way of

tackling the task in a systematic way is set out in *Worship Audit* (Grove Booklets Worship Series No. 133).

What the audit process involves

♦ Decide as a church to have a worship audit.

♦ Appoint a small group to oversee and run it.

♦ Invite an outside consultant to help if possible.

♦ Plan the programme – the whole process takes many months.

♦ Work out a biblical theology of worship – to form the basis for evaluating your worship.

♦ Discover the views of the congregation (and, if possible, those outside the congregation).

♦ Bring your theology and these views together and see what changes are needed.

♦ Make recommendations for change.

If an audit of your whole worship pattern seems too much to attempt, or unnecessary, you could start with a more limited audit – perhaps of all-age worship, or of evening worship. It's better to be realistic about what you can achieve, not least because a proper worship audit takes a lot of time and energy.

However, despite the risks and the effort involved, a complete worship audit can have enormously positive results.

● It enables more people to feel that their opinion has at least been heard and taken seriously.

● By engaging people in the debate it forces them to think about their own assumptions, and perhaps to reassess entrenched positions and stop caricaturing others.

● It makes people aware of other people's opinions and helps them to love and accept one another.

● It gives the chance to make long-overdue changes.

● It helps people to value the things that are good about their worship.

● It gives people a perspective beyond their own preferences.

● It can help people to grow as Christians.

This last point is worth stressing. The aim of the audit is *not* to make more people in the congregation happier with what happens in church on Sunday (even though they may be pleased that their opinion has been heard and valued). Nor is the aim solely to make non-Christians happy in church. Certainly, as we stressed at the end of the last chapter, we want to make our churches as accessible and welcoming to newcomers as possible. But it is a myth to think that the only thing preventing people from attending our churches is the worship, and that if we just make the worship easier to get into then people will come flooding in. The truth is that what will really attract them is the quality of our lives, what will impress them is the quality of our welcome, and what will keep them is the depth and reality of our love for one another

CHAPTER 3

and for them. Given love, people will often put up with dull and difficult worship – or else some congregations today would be even smaller than they are. Church is not a place we attend, but a family we belong to.

The aim of the audit, then, is not to make us or visitors happier, but to please God, for that is the purpose of worship. Of course, God is concerned about how we experience worship, and about how we welcome others. Our audit may lead us to broaden the range of services and worship styles, *not* in an attempt to suit more people but to enable us all to grow in appreciation of things which are not our natural preferences. The importance of balance and variety in worship is not a matter of pleasing more of the people more of the time – it is a *theological* issue of honouring God fully. Salvation is about wholeness and change, not stagnation and entrenchment. Trying to please everyone can easily result in 'lowest common denominator' worship which actually pleases no one. Trying to please God instead leads to a fullness, a diversity, and the ability to draw on different styles and traditions as appropriate, which allows each part of every act of worship to have integrity and to reflect the kingdom of God. We are called to experience and to appreciate new things which will enrich our own lives and the lives of others.

So a good worship audit will enable us to evaluate things from the

The aim of the audit is not to make us or visitors happier, but to please God.

perspective of the regular worshipper, from the perspective of those who are new or visiting and, above all, from the perspective of God himself.

Our own perspective is the easiest to consider. We can use a questionnaire to gather the views of the worshippers. Home groups or other groups can discuss the regular worship and feed their views back to the church leaders. You could call a special meeting and give people a chance to voice their opinions. Whatever you do, make sure that this gathering of *our* views is not regarded as the end of the audit, but as the beginning.

A worship audit can reveal a lot about our 'theology' of worship, and may show a need for more basic teaching. So it can help us to consider the deeper and more important issue of what God wants.

How people view worship

The comments people make as they leave a service reveal a lot about the subconscious assumptions they make about what worship actually is or should be about:

● Some see the worship as the **rite** itself. They are likely to say of the actual form of service: 'I much prefer a traditional service to this modern stuff,' or 'It's so lovely to use the Lord's Prayer in a form I can understand.' This is sometimes heard in churches from people who struggle with the change from traditional to modern forms of service. Familiarity breeds contentment, and people find the new forms less satisfying. But sometimes it's also a matter of theology. If you have grown up with the idea that real worship *is* the traditional form, then a modern replacement is not just *different* worship, it's not worship at all. No wonder people go away from church feeling let down and uneasy. Perhaps we are now seeing the same sort of attitudes in some people's reactions to so-called 'alternative' worship, which seems very different even to our modern concepts of liveliness.

● For some people the worship focuses on the **music**. They are likely to comment on the songs and hymns; whether they knew them, whether they liked them. For them a time of worship means a time of singing.
● For others the key thing is the **sermon**. The rest of the service not only serves as a build-up to the sermon, but is judged on whether the worshipper comes away feeling edified and built up.

Although people within each of these groups may disagree with each other, the real problems arise from different assumptions within a church about what worship is all about. This is especially dangerous when these assumptions remain hidden and unrecognized; all we see on the surface is that a discussion on worship will make a church council meeting a long one. Evaluation is clearly already happening – the task is to do that evaluation more directly and to base it on more solid foundations.

CHAPTER 3

Outsiders looking in

Gathering the views of those who are not regular worshippers is more difficult. You could ask those who you know will be coming for the first time to fill in a questionnaire. For example, couples coming for marriage preparation, or those coming to church as part of the preparation for the baptism of their child, or those who just come to festivals like Christmas. Beware though – you may not like what they tell you. They may prefer more traditional forms – or they may admit to not understanding anything. On the whole, the perspective of newcomers needs to be kept in the back of our minds, but never allowed to dominate. There are several reasons for this:

● By definition these are people who *don't* come, so it's hard to get a view based on long-term (rather than one-off) experience. Since the worship in most churches will vary from Sunday to Sunday in length, content, quality, etc., their views can be misleading.
● The church cannot devise and plan its regular worship around the needs of non-worshippers! Even the Willow Creek pattern of the 'church for the unchurched' has worship in the week for the committed Christians as well as the 'seeker services' for the unchurched. The concept of worshipping God (in any style) will be alien to someone who is not committed to Christ's lordship.
● Worship is a vital part of the church's calling in its own right. We must never allow it to become a mere means to the end of attracting others in.
● The imaginary visitor tends to get used as a pawn in a pitched battle raging *within* the church between those who like one thing rather than another. One group claims that 'no young people are going to come into our church until we scrap the organ and have more lively worship,' while another asserts that 'when visitors come we must have traditional hymns that they will know, not modern stuff they can't join in with'. So the supposed concern for the newcomer is hijacked to reinforce our own views.

CHAPTER 3

What does God think?

Getting a handle on God's perspective is the hardest of all. It's a shame we can't give him a questionnaire! It really needs some hard thinking and praying by a small group of people who together can wrestle with biblical and other insights, and discover a vision for what worship is all about. This needs to be seen by everyone as integral to the task of evaluating or auditing worship, and not as a bit of theory to be got out of the way quickly and then forgotten. The Bible has many things to say about worship that cut across some of our own cultural assumptions:

● Jesus tells us that self-fulfilment comes through self-denial and self-giving (Mark 8:34); we assume that self-fulfilment comes through self-indulgence, and so we talk wrongly of what we 'get out' of worship and of worship which 'meets our needs'.
● A common Old Testament model for understanding worship is sacrifice; our model is more likely to be drawn from the world of therapy or entertainment. So we may play down the sober elements of cost, and look instead for ways in which we might benefit from the worship.
● The prophets remind God's people of the need to link what we say and sing in worship with the way we live and order our society (Micah 6:8; Amos 5:14,15); we tend to see corporate worship as an escape from the realities of our daily lives.

There is plenty more biblical material to draw on, so it is important that your worship audit gives time to it in order to ensure that the criteria you use are biblical, and not the whims and preferences of individuals in the church (even if the majority of people share them). This is where the outside 'consultant' can be so useful. The Bible must be set free to guide people into thinking for themselves, and not used as a tool for manipulating the majority into a predetermined view.

HOW MANY MARKET RESEARCHERS HAVE VISITED YOU THIS YEAR?

MARKET RESEARCH

CHAPTER 3

What shall we ask them?

Your questionnaire needs to ask:

● How often do you come to which services?
● How long have you been coming?
● How welcome do you feel?
● How easily can you follow the service?
● How helpful are the service leaders?
● How do you rate the music?
● How helpful is the sermon?
● How helpful are the prayers and other elements?
● How well did the service prepare you for your life during the week?

Make sure the questionnaire covers every aspect of your worship. Break down the questions into simple sections and, whenever possible, get respondents to rate their score on a scale of 1-10, or give them multiple choice boxes to tick.

Leave space for their comments – and take them seriously.

A worship audit can be a painful experience as presuppositions are tested and the status quo challenged. However, this is nothing compared to the next stage – implementing any changes! The next chapters give some guidance about how to prepare for change and how to make it slightly less uncomfortable than tooth extraction.

'Yes, there have been adaptations to culture which have sold the gospel short. The historic Creeds of the church were largely forged as a response to undue adaptation in the form of heresy. At other times the church has risked the gospel by its refusal to adapt to change. When that happens it becomes simply an antiquarian ghetto. Nonetheless, the gospel has been taken to an extraordinarily rich diversity of cultures and survived as an expression of all that is most authentic about that culture.'

Robert Warren, Being Human, Being Church, Marshall Pickering, 1995, p 41

A model for worship based on the temple

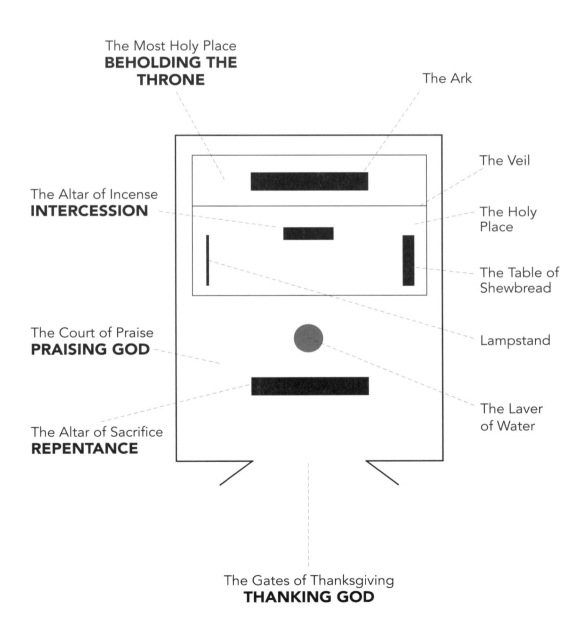

The Most Holy Place
BEHOLDING THE THRONE

The Ark

The Veil

The Altar of Incense
INTERCESSION

The Holy Place

The Table of Shewbread

The Court of Praise
PRAISING GOD

Lampstand

The Altar of Sacrifice
REPENTANCE

The Laver of Water

The Gates of Thanksgiving
THANKING GOD

Taken from A Kingdom of Priests, *(pp 4,6) by Mark Stibbe, published and copyright 1994 by Darton Longman and Todd Ltd and used by permission of the publishers.*

GROUP FOCUS

Aim

To prepare to take a worship audit in your church.

1. Bible base

Look up the following references. What do they tell you about God's perspective on our worship?

- 1 Chronicles 15, 16
- Psalm 42
- Psalm 115:2-8
- Psalm 145
- Amos 5:21-24
- Micah 6:6-8
- John 4:19-26
- 1 Corinthians 11:23-29
- Revelation 1:6
- Revelation 7:9-17
- Revelation 14:6-13
- Revelation 19:1-16

2. What matters to God?

Put the following in order of importance as you think *God* would see it as he considers your worship:

A quiet reflective atmosphere in church before the service begins	
The words of songs available on an overhead projector to free your hands for clapping	
Disabled access to your building, large print books for the visually impaired and a hearing aid loop	
A balance between old and new in the choice of songs	
Time for silence in the service itself	
A time for questions and discussion after the sermon	
'Pew Bibles' for everyone in a modern translation	

Compare your results with one another. How do you justify your choices?

3. Are we sitting comfortably?

Think about your own worship 'comfort zones' – what are the types of worship, or the parts of the service that make you feel safe and comfortable, and what are the things that make you feel vulnerable, exposed, challenged or ill at ease? Share your thoughts with others in the group, and be sensitive to one another. How typical are your views within the church?

4. Launch into audit

● What methods would you use for finding out the opinions of the regular congregation?
● What dangers or drawbacks would you need to be aware of in using the methods you have suggested?
● What ideas do you have for getting the views of newcomers and visitors?
● What would be the key things you would be looking for in the person or people you would choose as outside consultants?
● If you were to choose one area of your church's worship for a limited worship audit, what would you give priority to?

5. Aspects of worship

Think about what you are most likely to comment on after a service. Is it likely to be the form of service, the music, the sermon, or something else? Talk to each other about your answers. In your church, do you think there is a tendency to focus on one or other of these areas (or some other area) as being the *really* important aspect of worship?

CHAPTER 4

One step forward

Thinking about change

Having completed your worship audit you've decided that things are not perfect, and that there is perhaps a little room for improvement. How do you move forward from here? This chapter looks at some principles which may be helpful in thinking about change, and Chapter 5 contains some practical suggestions for its implementation.

There is a story of a little Welsh village chapel which saw substantial growth through its Welsh-language services, until the village was swallowed up by a post-war overspill estate. When it was suggested that the services should be held in English to cater for the large number of immigrants who had swamped the catchment area, the church refused the challenge and quietly aged and died. The suggestion that it was wrong to hold Welsh-language services raised too many hackles. In fact the real problem was that it was wrong to hold Welsh-language services *now*, even though in the past it had been perfectly appropriate.

Change as loss

An important breakthrough in my understanding of change came when I first heard someone remark that to most people change is usually perceived as loss. Often people actually *like* things the way they are; you can reason until the cows come home that it just isn't working, but at the end of the day the devil we know is better than the devil we don't. Therefore, if we even so much as suggest changing anything, people begin to feel bereaved and threatened. Even worse, if we dare to say that something needs changing it immediately implies that people were wrong to be doing it in the first place. In some cases this is undoubtedly true, but it isn't always.

Stepping stones

I find the picture of stepping stones helpful. Our previous parish was close to wild moorland, and on days off we were often to be found perched precariously in the middle of various rivers. I learned from this experience that the job of each stepping stone is to get us to the next and then be left behind. To stay on a stone because it's the 'right' one or even because it's the 'best' one is not going to get us anywhere at all. In church life this mentality prevents us from seeing ourselves as the pilgrim people of God. We can't stand safely on stone number five and say it was wrong to have been on stone number four. Number four got us to where we are now, and for that we need to be

In church life this mentality prevents us from seeing ourselves as the pilgrim people of God.

thankful. In time we must move on from number five to number six. Each stone did its job, but none of them provided a place to stay for ever.

Thus preaching, teaching and conversation can use this image gradually to pervade the church, a tactic which the prophet Isaiah uses to great effect in chapter 43 verses 16-21. 'This is what the Lord says – he who made a way through the [Red] sea...: "Forget the former things; do not dwell on the past. See, I am doing a new thing!"' Only when the past has been identified can it be forgotten. It wasn't *wrong*, it was just *then*, and this is *now*.

So it can be a useful exercise for a church to express its past, and to celebrate what has gone before, as an aid to moving on into the future by stepping onto the next stone.

Is there a way ahead?

But is there a stone to step on? We may feel a bit like the man who stopped in a complex London one-way system to ask directions from a passing Cockney, who announced, 'Sorry, guv, you can't get there from here.' This problem may be particularly acute if you have been to other churches which, in your perception, are perfect, or as near to perfect as makes no odds. Their high cost, state-of-the-art sound equipment, or their fifty-strong choir,

or their six separate worship teams can make you and the tone-deaf tuba player who make up your church's sole worship resource feel a little inadequate. The question 'Can we get there (or anywhere near there) from here?' seems very pertinent.

The answer is 'Yes, you can!', although it may take some time. Don't underestimate what can be achieved in five years, but don't overestimate what can be done in

one year. As the proverb says: 'How does an ant eat an elephant? In bite-sized bits.' That's the secret: break down the big problem which you can't solve into a set of smaller problems which you can at least begin to work on.

The church's values

The essential place to begin is the church's values which we talked about in Chapter 1. Are there ways in which, gradually and gently over a period of time, the whole culture of the church can be changed? Lots of small things can help, from the items put on the church council's agenda (and the order in which they appear) to throw-away comments like, 'Of course those who don't come to our church are more important than those who do' dropped into the conversation at appropriate moments. This kind of culture is caught more than it is taught; many church leaders remember the thrill when for the first time someone said back to them at a council meeting, 'Of course those who don't come to our church are more important than those who do'. In time everyone is saying it, and believing it too, without quite knowing where they got it from. This drip-feeding of different values can be a vital first step in softening up the ground so that practical change can begin and new things start to grow.

A sense of unease

This is another important pre-requisite for change. If everyone is in agreement with the way things are, there simply is no perceived need for anything to be different. But if people can be helped to see the flaws in the current state of things, and then shown something better, they will become less happy with the *status quo* and more open to something different. This can, of course, be quite a miserable time, if a church which thinks it is the bee's knees suddenly is confronted with the fact that it's not as wonderful as it thought. Indelicate handling of the situation by the leadership can lead to a deeper sense of threat and cause people to dig their heels in. Bursting someone's bubble without making them cry isn't easy, but fortunately this kind of bubble can be deflated gradually and gently.

Comparisons are often unhelpful, but to expose people to something which is closer to your vision than the current practice can be a helpful yet non-threatening way of creating discontent. For example, one minister deliberately started taking parties from his church to Spring Harvest, not because he particularly valued the teaching but because he wanted people to experience the kind of music in worship for which he had a vision. Experiencing the music of Graham Kendrick in a crowd of 5,000 dealt a death blow to their traditional hymnal; worship at home just didn't feel the same any more. This discontent, coupled with the bigger vision being experienced and not just talked about, provided real incentive to begin change. If your vision is that of better use of more traditional forms, then sampling the worship of well-trained, well-rehearsed choirs might have the same effect.

What this kind of thinking and action does is to create a culture which allows the church to think of itself as a pilgrim people, on the way somewhere but not there yet, aware of their imperfections but full of hope for a better future. They are deliberately on the move and therefore travelling light, unencumbered by tons of baggage from the past. Change-management experts agree that this outlook is a prime requisite for creative change.

A theology of failure

A third prerequisite is a theology of failure. Any change involves an element of risk, and therefore the possibility that we might get it wrong. This thought alone is capable of paralysing many churches, and if the creative discontent is handled badly so that people hear the leadership saying that as a church we're a failure, the problem is compounded.

The very word 'failure' is sometimes, wrongly, banned from people's vocabulary. Like many churches we have an annual Gift Day, when we set a target and try to give away the money we raise to causes chosen by

IF AT FIRST YOU DON'T SUCCEED— FAILURE MAY BE YOUR STYLE

CHAPTER 4

the church council. One year, for the first time ever, we fell spectacularly short of our target. You can't imagine the stick I got for telling the church we'd failed. 'Well, it was still a magnificent effort,' some said (which it was); 'It was better than nothing/last year's total/the parish down the road,' added others (again, all true). Anything, it seemed, to avoid using the dreaded 'F' word. To my mind, however, if you've expected to raise so much and you actually raise considerably less, that's failure, and pretty convincing failure at that. Moving the goalposts later to protect our self-esteem is fundamentally dishonest. So I had the difficult task of helping the church to face its failure instead of trying to wriggle out of it.

The good news is that we have a God who allows us to fail and still loves us. Sadly we live in a society in which people often give favour and love according to others' performance. 'Failures' don't gain friends or second chances. The church has sometimes taught the same thing about our Father God, so that to admit we've failed is to consign ourselves to his wrath. This false belief needs urgent correction.

We have a two-year-old daughter, who is learning the correct use of a potty. We don't expect her instantly to be perfect; we anticipate a period of experimentation! But we don't regard the occasional puddles on the floor as events which finish off our relationship, messy and inconvenient though they may be to us. Rather we delight in her continued growth and development, knowing (at times hoping!) that one day all will be well. If I, as an imperfect human father, can so delight in Vicki's 'failures', how much more does God not only cope with the failures of his church, but in a strange way almost rejoice in them? They are, after all, signs of life and progress, and he specializes in clearing up the messes his people sometimes make. To teach and live out a positive theology of failure is very liberating for a church and for its members, setting them free to experiment and grow without fear of being cast off by God.

Finally, how about identifying some goals to help along the journey? What could be done immediately with no hassle at all? What might you be doing by this time next year (remember that overestimation is the danger here)? Where might you be in five years' time (beware of underestimation)? And with what are you stuck, so that you can stop getting frustrated by it and work around it? To work through this can be very liberating, setting you free from unrealistic fantasies but at the same time filling you with hope and allowing you to plan for practical action.

Aim

To assess ways in which we could manage change in our church.

1. Bible base

a The Spirit of God is never still. What principles about change and God can you glean from these passages?

- Numbers 23:19
- Psalm 55:19
- Psalm 102:25-27
- Malachi 3:6
- Luke 5:36-39
- Acts 16:6-10
- Romans 7:6
- 1 Corinthians 9:19-23
- 2 Corinthians 5:17
- Revelation 21:5

b The past was of great importance for Bible writers. Why? How might we adopt similar attitudes? Look at Psalms 44, 106 and 107.

2. Look back in appreciation

What have been your major milestones (or stepping stones) in the past? How were they celebrated, and how easy has it been to move on from there? Compile a brief biography of your church, and use it as a basis for a service of thanksgiving for your church's past.

3. Assess your failure

Think of a major failure in the life of your church. How was it handled, and how did people feel about it? Do you feel now that it has been owned by the church, or swept under the carpet? Have any lessons been learnt, and are there people who are still hurting from it? Is any action needed? What, and by whom?

GROUP FOCUS

4. Identify what needs changing

a With your group, use the following chart to fill in ten things you'd like to change about your worship.

	What needs changing?	A/B/C/X
1		
2		
3		
4		
5		
6		
7		
8		
9		
10		

(You may *not* continue on a separate sheet: ten only!)

b Explain to one another *from your values* why you think these ten things need changing, and alter the list as you do so if necessary, until you can all agree about it.

c Then go down the list and identify what things you could do tomorrow, at little or no cost, and with minimal opposition (for example, moving the lectern to the other side so that people can see better). Put a letter 'A' against them.

Then decide what you could do fairly quickly after convincing others it was a good idea and finding the money (for example, producing your own user-friendly service cards). Mark them with a 'B'.

Thirdly, identify those things which would be long-term projects, but which might be possible within, say, a few years (building a new baptistry or coffee area might come into this category). Give those things a 'C'.

Finally, mark with an 'X' those things with which to all intents and purposes you're stuck, things that it's a waste of time even worrying about. Just work around them.

d Now go and do some of your 'A's.

Making the change

Policy decisions

Change-management is a highly complex subject about which much has been written. What we can do, however, is look at some simple principles which churches have found effective in developing their worship. There must be a will to change, at least among sufficient people to form a 'critical mass' which can set things moving; if not, go back a step and continue with the value-changing mentioned earlier. To press ahead with radical change against the will of the church is unlikely to be helpful in the long term.

So what might we actually do? First we'll look at some major policy decisions that need to be made, then we'll look at some possibilities for change.

Who plans it?

It is a wise leader who involves others in decision-making, particularly over such an emotive issue as worship. The word 'committee' may have too many negative connotations of talking-shops which take no action, but some kind of an evaluation and planning group – as recommended in *In Tune With Heaven*, the report of the Archbishops' Commission on Church Music (London: Church House/Hodder and Stoughton, 1992), pages 189, 197 – is useful in most settings. The people invited onto the group may be chosen to reflect the diversity of the church, but those whose only role in life seems to be to obstruct everything should be excluded. After all, the purpose of the group is to discern the way forward. If you have completed a worship audit it may be appropriate for the group responsible for that to move on to provide leadership in implementing the changes recommended. Alternatively, you may want to constitute a different group to take things on from there.

How much change?

Most churches have more than one service each Sunday, and some have as many as six. A policy decision needs to be made as to how many of them should or can be changed. Those opting for a 'menu' approach, in which different services have different worship styles from which people pick and choose what they like, often justify themselves by saying that people have a right to worship in their own way, and that the church is there to provide something for everyone. On the other hand opponents of this view say that it can encourage selfishness

CHAPTER 5

... the church is there to provide something for everyone.

and consumerism, may provide forms of worship which help people to hide from God rather than to encounter him, and wears out the clergy! It is also capable of being taken to ridiculous extremes – do we have one service for those who like the confession at the beginning and another for those who like it later on?

This question is of major importance, and cannot be ducked. Often, though, pragmatism triumphs. However much we may feel that such-and-such a service needs renewing, it would be practically impossible to do anything without World War Three breaking out, so let's leave well alone and work on what *can* be changed.

How far should change go?

Tied in with this is the question of

just how much we change those bits we do want to change. Again, a policy decision is needed early on, for example as to whether we are going to abolish hymns and hymn-books altogether and go whole-heartedly for OHP-driven worship songs, or whether we want a mixture of both. And if the proposed renewal of our worship is so radical that it conflicts with our denominational values and norms, we have some hard questions to answer about whether we still belong. Would an Anglican church, for example, which decides to abandon liturgy altogether in favour of spontaneous worship, have the right any longer to call itself 'Anglican'?

These are big questions, and policy issues like these need careful agreement before any practical changes are made. But having decided what we want to do, here are some ideas for how we might go about doing it.

Explain your proposals

As I look back on my childhood, I reckon that I had a pretty good relationship with my parents (and still do). I felt basically secure with them, and sure of their love. But on those occasions when I did feel upset and angry, there was often a common factor: I didn't understand why they were doing what they were doing. The same is true with God: the times when we get most hurt or upset are very often when we simply can't see how this is part of his great eternal plan for us. If, like him, we could see the end from the beginning, we'd probably take it all much more calmly, but so often we simply have to trust that he does know what he's doing. That's not easy when we're going through the mill.

From Job's point of view disaster after meaningless disaster suddenly struck. The readers, however, are given a glimpse into a different realm, to witness the interaction between God and Satan which is behind it all. Many of the changes which people experience in church life feel a bit like that. As far as they are concerned disaster has afflicted their dearly-loved services from out of the blue. Of course, the church council has good reasons for what it is doing, but to the mere mortals in the pews such reasons are invisible. So it is important to let people in on your planning at an early stage, carefully explaining what and why certain things are going to happen. If people can see a reason for the change they are far more likely to accept it, and even in time get used to it. And above all, they need to be helped to see how the proposed changes grow out of your values as a church.

Use experimentation and feedback

Most people are willing to try things for a limited period if they don't believe they will necessarily go on for ever. To explain to a church council why change is needed, and that this

particular idea might be the right way ahead, but that we're not certain and need to run with it for a while to see, is, in many places, likely to be greeted with a positive response. The leadership needs to respect this willingness to suck-it-and-see by not abusing the experiment; into the original contract should be built the stopping date and the meeting of the council for reviewing it.

Use the church's year

The Lord, in his wisdom and mercy, has given two major gifts to the church: Lent and August. These are times when good Christians expect to be miserable and absent respectively, and so can be used for creative experimentation with little opposition. I mentioned earlier a church whose pilgrimage in worship took a major step forward when they gained permission to use a music group during communion one August. They stopped once September arrived, but the experiment was so successful that the church council quickly made it a permanent arrangement.

Pinch ideas shamelessly!

Yes, of course you're trying to develop a worship style which is rightly yours, but it is often easier to start with something nearly right and tweak it a bit than it is to create from scratch. So how about sending your worship group members on fact-finding missions to other churches (of all types) to cull some good practices and possible ideas?

CHAPTER 5

Add, don't change

It will often cause fewer ripples if something is added elsewhere in the life of the church than if you blow to bits your main Sunday act of worship. Many churches have found new life through Sunday evening 'Celebration' services where those who like that sort of thing can experiment with Rave, Taizé, Iona, Toronto, or whatever, while the normal services continue untouched. My experience is that they don't remain untouched for ever, since the positive things people have experienced elsewhere begin to overflow and make their mark on the 'normal' services, albeit in a less dramatic way.

Little by little

Personally, my idea of excitement is a take-away vindaloo and a video of *The Simpsons*, so I've never done anything remotely as dangerous as rock-climbing. But a more adventurous friend taught me an important principle about change from his experiences up various mountains. The idea, apparently, is that you have four points of contact with the rock face (five if you count your teeth). You only let go of one of them at a time, and only when you have got a firm grip on a new foot- or hand-hold do you venture to move the next limb. Progress is thus slow but safe: leaping from rock to rock in the style of a goat is definitely discouraged!

The wise leader recognizes that worshippers too need some security if they are to move on. To arrive at church one week to find the pews swapped for scatter-cushions, the hymn-books replaced by an OHP, a rock-band instead of the choir and incense sticks where the candles used to be may well cause the congregation to feel just a little bit as though they were dangling in mid-air. So introduce changes gradually (there's that strategy again) and allow people to become secure with one thing before you change something else.

Review honestly

It is a hard thing for a leader to see that their pet idea, which they have

The idea is that you have four points of contact with the rock face (five if you count your teeth).

nursed carefully through church councils and worship group meetings, has been an absolute flop in practice, but it does need seeing. A good leader will develop over the years the practice of abandoning things which simply don't work, rather than sticking to them because they ought to. This pragmatism requires a lot of grace and not a few apologies, but the eating of humble pie can be made a lot easier if the idea is presented in the first place as an experiment. It's much harder to climb down in front of the church council if you sold the idea originally as the answer to every problem of the universe.

Facts, not feelings

Tied in with the review system is the need accurately to record statistics which will let you know how things were, as opposed to how they felt. We introduced for a one-year experimental period a monthly non-eucharistic Family Service. At the end of the year we decided to stop it, because it *felt* as if it wasn't working. But then one of the church council members, who enjoys drawing graphs on his computer, did some work with the service register and showed us clearly that the attendance was regularly higher that Sunday than on the other three, and that a large proportion of our growth had come through that service. To stop it would have closed down a major area of mission, and we nearly did so purely on impressions. We need to have a business-like

approach so that we can make informed decisions.

Treat one another with grace

American preacher Tony Campolo tells the story of a church in the USA, where the preacher is usually encouraged enthusiastically by the congregation while the sermon is going on, with cries of 'Hallelujah!', 'Preach it, man!' and so on. On this occasion, however, it was not going well. The preacher, stumbling over his words and digging himself deeper and deeper into theological holes, was greeted with a deafening silence from the congregation, until the voice of a little old lady from somewhere near the back broke through the polite confusion with the heartfelt prayer, 'Help him, Jesus!'

Those of us who have the painful privilege of being 'up front' in church services know only too well that feeling. But I am always amazed how many members of the congregation think we're totally oblivious to the embarrassing mess we're making of things, and feel the need to tell us afterwards in the porch how terrible it all was. If it felt bad out there, how on earth do they think it felt for me having to preside over it?

Anything new in worship, music, liturgy; different people reading or praying out loud; drama or dance; it all has the potential for going horribly wrong, at least to start with.

CHAPTER 5 _____

But if we are the pilgrim people of God on a risky journey together, we'll learn to deal graciously with those whose well-intentioned attempts at worship didn't quite come off, rather than treating them as the enemy who has set out to inflict such pain on us. I'd rather hear, 'Help him, Jesus!' than 'Smite him, Jesus!'

Change is rarely easy. It is never painless, but it can cause less pain if it is handled carefully. Those of us responsible for this workbook have written as those on the same journey, and we offer it to the church with the prayer that our worship may be a joy to us, an inspiration to those not yet quite with us, and a delight to God, for whose glory the church, and all creation, exist.

Aim

To identify ways in which we could move forward.

1. Bible base

How did God's people in the Old Testament prepare for big advances? Make a list of the principles you can identify, and discuss how you should apply them locally.

- Exodus 12, 13
- Deuteronomy 1:1-36
- Joshua 1–4

2. Think through how to make the change

a Who leads?

Do you have a 'worship group', as mentioned in the text? If so, how does it work? Are the right people on it? If not, how might one work, and who might you have on it?

b How much change?

Do you run a 'menu' church? How do you feel about that? Are there some parts of the worshipping life of your church which you leave out of your thinking? Set up a role-play between, for example, a hymn-book and an OHP acetate, or an organ and a synthesizer, each putting their case for being changed or left alone.

c How far can you go?

Your fairy godmother (or guardian angel if you want to be theological) has granted you three wishes for your worship: one for Lent, one for August, and one for an extra weekly Sunday service. What would you choose to do? And why?

d Explaining the process

Choose one of the plans marked with a 'C' from the exercise in the previous chapter. Pretend you have decided to go ahead and do it, and devise a strategy for explaining the decision to the congregation so that it will win their approval.

e Reviewing services

What mechanisms do you have for reviewing your services? How well do you ensure that your opinions are based on factual information?

3. And finally...

Talk together about how helpful or otherwise you have found this course. Is there anything to show for it, or has it just been an interesting intellectual exercise? Plan to meet to ask the same question in a year's time.